Theos Friends' Programme

GN01048790

Theos is a public theology think tank which seeks to
about the role of faith and belief in society.

We were launched in November 2006 with the suppo
Canterbury, Dr Rowan Williams and the Cardinal Arch
Cardinal Cormac Murphy-O'Connor.

We provide

- high-quality research, reports and publications;
- an events programme;
- news, information and analysis to media companies,
  parliamentarians and other opinion formers.

We can only do this with your help!

Theos Friends receive complimentary copies of all Theos publications, invitations
to selected events and monthly email bulletins.

Theos Associates receive all the benefits of Friends and in addition are invited
to attend an exclusive annual dinner with the Theos Director and team.

If you would like to become a Friend or an Associate, please detach
or photocopy the form to the right, and send it with a cheque to Theos
for the relevant amount.   Thank you.

Yes, I would like to help change public opinion!
I enclose a cheque payable to Theos for: ☐ **£60** (Friend) ☐ **£300** (Associate)

☐ Please send me information on how to give by standing order/direct debit

Name _____

Address _____

_____ Postcode _____

Email _____

Tel _____

Data Protection Theos will use your personal data to inform you of its activities.
If you prefer not to receive this information please tick here. ☐

By completing you are consenting to receiving communications by telephone and email.
Theos will not pass on your details to any third party.

Please return this form to:
Theos | 77 Great Peter Street | London | SW1P 2EZ
S: 97711:   D: 36701:

Theos

The public theology think tank

The public theology think tank

what Theos is

Theos is a public theology think tank which exists to undertake research and provide commentary on social and political arrangements. We aim to impact opinion around issues of faith and belief in society. We were launched in November 2006 with the support of the Archbishop of Canterbury, Dr Rowan Williams, and the Cardinal Archbishop of Westminster, Cardinal Cormac Murphy-O'Connor. Our first report *"Doing God": A Future for Faith in the Public Square* examined the reasons why faith will play an increasingly significant role in public life.

what Theos stands for

Society is embarking on a process of de-secularisation. Interest in spirituality is increasing across western culture. Faith is on the agenda of both government and the media. In the arts, humanities and social sciences there are important intellectual developments currently taking place around questions of values and identity. Theos speaks into this new context. Our perspective is that faith is not just important for human flourishing and the renewal of society, but that society can only truly flourish if faith is given the space to do so. We reject notions of a sacred-secular divide.

what Theos works on

Theos undertakes research across a wide range of subject areas. We analyse social and political change and offer interesting new angles and alternative perspectives on the issues that matter.

what Theos provides

Theos provides:

- a research and publishing programme;
- conferences, seminars and lectures;
- news, information and analysis to media companies and other opinion formers, with a one-stop information line available to journalists;
- regular email bulletins;
- other related activities.

In addition to our independently driven work, Theos provides research, analysis and advice to individuals and organisations across the private, public and not-for-profit sectors. Our unique position within the think tank sector means that we have the capacity to develop proposals that carry values – with an eye to demonstrating what really works. Our staff and consultants have strong public affairs experience, an excellent research track record and a high level of theological literacy.

www.theosthinktank.co.uk

The Politics of Christmas

Stephen R Holmes

Published by Theos in 2011
© Theos

ISBN-13 978-0-9562182-7-8

Some rights reserved – see copyright licence for details

For further information and subscription details please contact:

Theos
Licence Department
77 Great Peter Street
London
SW1P 2EZ

T 020 7828 7777
E hello@theosthinktank.co.uk
www.theosthinktank.co.uk

contents

executive summary

Our political debate stops at Christmas. Historically, this is because the Victorians re-invented Christmas as a time to celebrate the family and domesticity, with a gentle leaven of personal charity, and so it became a festival that excluded politics. Up to the early nineteenth century, Christmas had often been celebrated with anarchic reversals of authority structures.

If we read the accounts of the birth of Jesus in the Bible, however, we will find this silencing of politics very odd. These stories, at the heart of what Christmas is supposed to be about, offer a picture of the world in which politics affects the domestic life of ordinary families at every turn: Mary and Joseph are only in Bethlehem because of a census intended to regularise taxation records; they rapidly become asylum seekers in Egypt, fleeing oppression by the local political authority, King Herod. The story suggests to us that we cannot easily separate domesticity and politics, and that any celebration of the family will inevitably be political.

More than that, however, the biblical stories of the birth of Jesus are set at a time of political unrest. Palestine at the time has fairly recently been occupied by Rome, and resentment and talk of revolution are everywhere. Read against this background, the account of the birth of Jesus in Luke's Gospel in particular suggests that this birth is understood by those around, and by the gospel writer, as marking God's decisive intervention in the political realm, which will lead to the overthrow of the empire and the setting free of the people. The Christmas story is a story of God's interference in, and transformation of, the political order.

The birth of Jesus was a political event, through and through. Our celebration of Christmas should therefore be political also.

we don't do politics at Christmas

We don't do politics at Christmas. There is no need for a report to argue that; we all know it. By universal, if unspoken, consent, the otherwise-endless partisan debate shuts down, newspapers spike their guns, and broadcasters, usually so ready to host and fuel a political spat, switch to anodyne musical items or feel-good human interest stories. For one day, at least, our political machine closes down.

As Prime Minister, Gordon Brown took to issuing messages to the Christian community at Christmas and Easter. These were not political messages, however, but part of a general engagement with faith groups in British society; he would similarly greet Muslims at Eid-al-Fitr and Hindus at Diwali. David Cameron has continued in the same way, although he did not make any comment last Christmas. Instead, his message to the Christian community was given at Easter, paralleling his greetings delivered to the Jewish community on Rosh Hashanah, and so on. His more political broadcast was timetabled for New Year, deliberately avoiding the Christmas holiday itself. (There is also a tradition of a Prime Ministerial Christmas greeting to British troops serving abroad, but it is of course similarly apolitical.) Our political leaders themselves choose to silence the political debate at Christmas.

This is not confined to recent years. One of the more iconic tales in contemporary Christmas folklore is the story of the 1914 'Christmas Armistice', when British and German troops ceased fighting and met between the trench lines for games of football and other fraternising.[1] At the time this was seen as a worryingly subversive event: if the troops discovered that the enemy were people just like them, it was feared, they would be less ready to fight. (A year later, whilst some local ceasefires happened, they were far less widespread, not least due to specific and threatening instructions from the military commands on both sides.)

In popular imagination, however, the event has become a celebration of the mythical power of the Christmas season to transcend politics. Even in times of war, the impetus to put aside conflict in favour of recognition of our common humanity is too strong to be resisted, or so we have told ourselves. This story is so well-known that it is even available for lampooning in popular comedy, as for instance in the powerful final episode of the television series *Blackadder Goes Forth*, where in the preparation for an assault 'over the top', Baldrick (played by Tony Robinson) asks in poignant tones if others remember the

Christmas football match. Captain Blackadder (Rowan Atkinson) replies: "Remember it? How could I forget it? I was never offside. I could not *believe* that decision."

My purpose in this report is certainly not to condemn this annual seasonal silence in the otherwise ceaseless political debate. I suspect, in fact, that a more extended and/or more regular shutting down would benefit not just the health and family lives of politicians, and of the journalists who report on them, but also the broader engagement of (party) politics in society. That which is unceasing, or nearly so, after all, is in constant danger of becoming stale. Instead, I want to ask why the one brief silence we have in the year comes at Christmas, and whether the timing is appropriate. Is the Christmas season properly apolitical?

That is certainly what the British think. Theos and the polling company ComRes asked a demographically representative sample of over 2,000 British adults in autumn 2011 what they thought Christmas was about. Domesticity and charity topped the charts by a considerable margin. Five in six people (83%) agreed that "Christmas is about spending time with family and friends" (only 6% disagreed), and three in five (62%) agreed that "Christmas is a time when we should be generous to people less fortunate than ourselves" (8% disagreed). A sizeable minority (41%) agreed that "Christmas is about celebrating that God loves humanity", and about the same number said they thought that "Christmas is a good excuse for taking time off but doesn't really have any meaning today." Rather less popular was the idea that "Christmas is a time when we should challenge poverty and economic injustice" (34% agreed) and bottom of the list was the idea that "Christmas is a time when we should challenge political oppression around the world", to which only 19% agreed and 30% disagreed. The message was clear: domesticity and charity yes, religion maybe, politics and economics no.

It is worth noting, if only in passing, that those people who called themselves Christian were not much different in their opinions. Perhaps not surprisingly, Christians were more likely than the average to agree that Christmas is "about celebrating that God loves humanity" (58% vs. 41%), and that it is a time "when we should be generous to people less fortunate than ourselves" (68% vs 62%). However, there was next to no difference between Christians and non-Christians in terms of their political and economic understanding of Christmas. Whether or not one does politics at, or sees politics in, Christmas appears to have little to do with whether or not one calls oneself a Christian.

Even seemingly politically-significant Christmas moments are, when we examine them closely, at best ambiguous. In 1971, for instance, John Lennon and Yoko Ono made a lasting contribution to our Christmas soundtrack with their single, 'Happy Xmas, War is Over'. The song was a protest against the continuing military involvement of the United States in Vietnam, and so was an intervention in a pressing, and highly-charged, political debate. The form of the intervention, however, was striking: the lyrics suggested that peace and goodwill between all people was a part of the essential message of Christmas: "And so happy Christmas, for black and for white, for yellow and red ones, let's stop all the fight…" This was not a plea against the injustice of the war, so much as an appeal to a Christmas spirit that should transcend war. (John Prine's 'Sam Stone', released the same year, was a much more direct political comment, emphasising the injustice of the lack of support for returning veterans.) Christmas is not a time for political comment; at most, it is a time for invocations of a higher vision.

History inevitably remains messy. Christine Agius has explored several interesting stories of how the celebration of Christmas has been appropriated in support of 'the war effort',[2] including accounts of changes in American Christmas celebrations post-9/11, and the massive, and at least somewhat successful, German National Socialist effort of the 1930s to recast Christmas as a nationalist festival, celebrating at once the coming of the Messiah and the coming of the Führer.[3] Agius's reading of these events, however, relies on an assumption, which she clearly regards as general, that:

> Christmas is normally associated with notions of goodwill, generosity, and empathy for those less fortunate. It is a time of family gatherings, with a shared understanding of returning to a particular tradition that is celebrated within the family unit (be that nuclear or extended) whilst others do the same.[4]

Agius assumes an apolitical, domestic, and nostalgic celebration of Christmas as normal, and uses this to critique the politicisation of the festival in times of conflict as a distortion of the 'true meaning' of Christmas. If, sometimes, in times of heightened national threat, we do politics at Christmas, we should not; this is not what Christmas is for.

We might ask the question, though, is this broad cultural agreement correct? Is Christmas really a festival that, if only we understood its essential nature, would encourage us to cease, even if only temporarily, our conflicts, political and military? That question is the burden of this report.

The biggest problem in offering an answer is that the 'essential nature' of Christmas is rather complex. The festival we now celebrate (where 'we' means twenty-first century British people) is the product of a long, rich, and occasionally controversial cultural development. In the remainder of this chapter, I will chart (some aspects of) the recent course of that development, in an attempt to explain why and how we have depoliticised Christmas in our popular imagination. The result will be a suggestion that politics is not precisely excluded from the modern Christmas, but is only acceptable in certain, attenuated, forms. Following that, I will turn to the foundational stories of the festival, the narratives of the birth of Jesus Christ found in the New Testament, and ask about the extent to which they support this modern and depoliticised Christmas narrative.

the Victorian invention of Christmas

The first task, then, is to explore the development of our modern celebration of Christmas. I will focus on Britain, although inevitably some American and European history will intrude. Cultural historians talk of (and disagree about) 'the Victorian invention of Christmas'.[5] (The disagreements turn on whether our modern Christmas celebrations are a Victorian invention, or a Victorian selection and reconfiguration of earlier elements; the debate, whilst interesting, changes little of my argument in this report.) In the middle of the nineteenth century, in Britain, but also in the United States, the celebration of Christmas was revived (in many places the festival was almost ignored up to that time[6]). At the same time, however, the festival was reconfigured as a celebration of domesticity, where once it had been a public occasion for (temporary) subversion of the social order.

A telling example of this is found in the famous American Christmas poem, 'Twas the night before Christmas,' written by Clement Clarke Moore in 1822. This poem has become a central part of the American festivities, still being read every Christmas Eve by many families. The narrator of the poem begins with an account of a household settled down for the night, "Not a creature was stirring, not even a mouse". Suddenly, "out on the lawn there arose such a clatter, / I sprang from the bed to see what was the matter." At the time of composition, in the USA, a clatter on the lawn late on Christmas Eve would have meant one thing only: youths, probably drunken, roaming the neighbourhood demanding gifts from respectable householders.[7] Moore's narration of the experience of instead discovering St Nicholas, or 'Santa Claus,'[8] is an early part of a far-reaching reconstruction of the Christmas festival away from a moment in which the established political order was reversed to a festival celebrating domesticity and the family.

At least some regiments of the British Army retain a tradition once universal that, on Christmas Day, the officers serve the other ranks in the Mess; further, officers would replace men on guard duty and similar. This is an echo of an older Christmas tradition, where social structures were inverted on the one day, or for longer, and tenants could demand gifts from their landlords, or even make law-like decisions, which would stand for the duration of the season of misrule. Inevitably, as Moore's poem suggests, this often became a moment, even if a limited one, of threatening and antisocial behaviour. This Christmas tradition was profoundly political: whether one reads it as a ritual subversion of the social order, pregnant with revolutionary possibilities, or as a 'safety-valve', a moment when the working classes were permitted to let off steam so that they would remain docile and subservient for the rest of the year, the politics of Christmas were both obvious and profound.

At the beginning of the nineteenth century then, Christmas was, or at least could be (local traditions varied widely), a political moment not dissimilar to an adult version of the childish 'trick or treat' games of the contemporary Halloween (but profoundly more threatening because it involved adults not children). Moore's narrator would have been genuinely fearful: gangs of young adults, roaming the streets, careless of assumed social structures and property norms – the Christmas Moore knew was a situation not too far removed from the English urban riots of the past summer. If Christmas revelry did not often extend to quite such wanton destruction and looting, it was only because the unspoken ties of social order restrained even drunken youths. There must have been, however, a constant fear for any local householder, that celebrations of this sort could turn very ugly. Christmas in 1820 was, where it was celebrated, highly charged and political; now we don't do politics at Christmas. What has changed?

In Britain it is a novelist rather than a poet who is credited with reinventing Christmas; in place of Moore's sight of Santa Claus, our iconic literary picture is Scrooge's vision of three ghosts. Peter Ackroyd, in his biography of Charles Dickens, makes so bold as to claim that his subject "almost singlehandedly created the modern idea of Christmas."[9] Dickens' Christmas is not precisely apolitical - Scrooge's attitude to the plight of (the family of) his employee, Bob Cratchit, is transformed utterly by the ghostly visitations – but the politics is carefully circumscribed. Personal charity is a proper yuletide attitude, and so gifts to Cratchit and his family are appropriate, but there is no place in the tale for querying the basis of the economic and social system that impoverishes Bob Cratchit in the first place or condemns Tiny Tim to a precarious life of dependence on random kindnesses just because of his disability. The transformed Scrooge is more generous, but no more political. He gives gifts to those in need, but does not begin to imagine challenging the system that keeps them needy.

> A Christmas Carol *was published in December 1843 and tapped into, indeed significantly shaped, a cultural rediscovery of Christmas traditions that had been going on for perhaps two decades.*

A Christmas Carol was published in December 1843 and tapped into, indeed significantly shaped, a cultural rediscovery of Christmas traditions that had been going on for perhaps two decades. The renaissance originally turned on the recovery of traditional Christmas songs – Dickens' choice of title is significant – which had begun with Davies Gilbert's publication of Some Ancient Christmas Carols in 1822. Gilbert's interest was in the ancient culture of his native Cornwall, but he started a fashion for the recovery of old Christmas songs, which widened into an interest in the ways in which Christmas had once been celebrated. TK Hervey published The Book of Christmas in 1836, exploring a variety of older traditions and lamenting their decline. For Hervey, the loss of the traditional celebrations of Christmas was a result of the far-reaching disruption of British social life caused by massive migrations to the cities. For his readers, Christmas would be reinvented as a moment of domestic bliss, when the doors of the house could be bolted against the uncertain and rapidly changing politics and economics of the world outside, and symbols recovered from a rural past could be deployed to insist on the essentially unchanging nature of our ways of life.

Christmas as a celebration of domesticity

This celebration of domesticity, and particularly of the family, has become a central part of the modern Christmas. Survey data suggest that we are more ready to describe Christmas as a 'family' festival than as a religious one.[10] As noted above, an overwhelming majority of people see "Christmas as about spending time with family and friends". Another Theos/ComRes survey, from December 2010, saw 61% of people agreeing that "Christmas is mainly for children." Anthropologists who pay particular attention to the varied modes of celebration of Christmas in contemporary Britain suggest that one of the most constant factors is the central place of the (nuclear) family in our rituals of celebration.[11] Patterns of hospitality and (particularly) of shared meals; practices of gift-exchange, and the value of the gifts exchanged; and many other concrete features of the way people choose to celebrate Christmas, all emphasise the importance of a certain, fairly restricted, set of family ties. Grandparents will typically be invited into the nuclear home; aunts, uncles, and cousins occasionally, but less typically; wider family members rarely. Token gifts may be given widely, including to professional acquaintances and friends, but valuable gifts will generally be restricted to parents, children, and siblings.

In this context, I reflect on the various churches of which I have been a member. In each there was one, or a very small number of people who would open their homes on Christmas Day to members of the community who were separated from family – often, but not exclusively, students from overseas. Both the sense that motivated this practice, that it is somehow tragic to dine alone on Christmas Day, and the almost heroic sacrifice that others saw this as, point to the centrality of the family in the celebration of Christmas. As the poet Wendy Cope has it, in one of several humorous reflections on Christmas she has published, "the whole business is unbelievably dreadful, if you're single."[12]

Christmas has become a celebration of domesticity, of the close family. It is precisely because of this, I suggest, that statistics concerning divorce and family break-up peak each year just after Christmas: on the one hand, traditional practices force family members to spend considerable time together, potentially highlighting an existing failure of a relationship in such a way that it can no longer be ignored; on the other, and perhaps more insidiously, Christmas traditions imagine and project a perfect family life, and so challenge as inadequate the life of every real family, which is of course multiply imperfect, as all lived reality is. Faced with an idealised vision, it is easier to despair of messy reality and to decide to give up on family life altogether.

Is a celebration of domesticity apolitical? The answer, probably, depends on the precise form of domesticity that is celebrated. Whilst extreme political positions that reject the place of the family in society occasionally arise in history, virtually all mainstream politics would see family life, broadly construed, as something to be celebrated and supported. The family, where it exists, is a primary component of social stability, a crucial context for the education and socialisation of young people, and an enormous contributor to the offering of social care. Equally, however, the family can become politicised through debates over the extent or limits of what constitutes a proper 'family'. (Do gay/lesbian couples count? Do mixed-race couples count? What about adoption, or serial monogamy, or co-habitation without marriage? All of these issues have been live in in my experience in the last few years; some in national political debate; others in local contexts in which I have worked which, admittedly, may have been unusual.) Dickens, and those around him who imagined and constructed the Victorian Christmas, were untroubled by such questions. They knew what a 'family' was; they believed – perhaps wrongly – that their definition was timeless and apolitical; and they made Christmas a festival of the family.

charity in the Victorian Christmas

Dickens' great novella was not the only element that contributed to the formation of the Victorian Christmas, of course. To take only one other example, Prince Albert's introduction of the tradition of a Christmas tree in 1841 was enormously significant in shaping the visible modes of celebration of the festival. Competing legends grew up around Albert's tree (was it a remembrance of St Boniface's destruction of a pagan sacred tree in his evangelisation of the Germanic tribes?), but all of them reached back in time to what Christmas, and what society, had once been, a Romantic vision of a timeless rural idyll that industrialisation and urbanisation had destroyed.

In this myth of what had been, social relations were deeply stratified, but in a fundamentally benign way. Those higher up the social and economic pyramid recognised that they inhabited the same society as their 'inferiors', and so felt a sense of responsibility towards those below them. Personal charity was thus built in to the (imagined) social structure, and those who were poor or disabled or otherwise disadvantaged would be cared for because they were a part of a caring society. The relationship between Scrooge and Cratchit could never quite mirror this mythical relationship of a country squire to his tenants, a relationship that the Victorians sometimes imagined to have been close to perfect. However, Christmas could and would become part of an ideological construction that called those who had benefited from the new economic and social arrangements to ape, however imperfectly, the imagined virtue of the ancient squire, and to offer private charity to their subordinates, particularly in the Christmas season. Scrooge's change of heart towards the Cratchits would become a parable of how properly to celebrate Christmas.

The first Christmas card, designed by J C Horsley and printed in 1843 (the same year as the publication of *A Christmas Carol*) illustrated this point powerfully. Its central image, placed above the greeting, was of a middle class family enjoying the Christmas feast – a further reinforcement of the centrality of domesticity – but to either side were images of charity: paupers being given food on the left, and paupers being given clothing on the right. The indulgence of the Christmas festivities, the card suggests, is legitimised by a demonstrated concern for the poor that is also a central part of the celebration of the season. The excess of goods that the middle-class Victorian family was presumed to enjoy should be spent both in domestic feasting, and in giving charity to those who did not enjoy such an excess.

The Victorian Christmas, then, was political in the sense that charity towards the needy (or at least the 'deserving' needy) was a component part of it. The ideal celebration of the season recognised that there were those in Victorian Britain who, through no fault of their own, were in desperate financial need; to celebrate Christmas properly was to act to

> *The Victorian Christmas was political in the sense that charity was a component part of it.*

meet this need. Factory owners who read Dickens instituted seasonal gifts of food – often enough a goose or, amongst Dickens' American readers, a turkey – to all their workers; Christmas boxes for delivery boys, postmen, and domestic servants became a part of the ideology of the season. Christmas was a time for counting blessings, recalling briefly that others knew less benediction, and giving something to assuage their need, however temporarily, before shutting the door against the world to enjoy the family celebration. Of course, the poor and needy would never be invited to share the family table: domesticity remained the primary mode of celebration of the season.

Our modern charity Christmas appeals retain something of this understanding. The national homelessness charity Crisis does excellent work throughout the year, but is able to leverage the continuing power of the Victorian Christmas to expand its services massively over the holiday. No doubt Crisis would not agree, but patterns of giving and volunteering suggest that many of its seasonal supporters take the view that someone sleeping rough at Christmas is somehow more tragic, or more troubling to the conscience of the onlooker, than that same person sleeping rough any other night of the year. (Crisis, it should be said, do excellent work in linking the extra provision they are able to make over the Christmas period to long term help for those clients who choose to access it.) Internationally, the proliferation of 'shoebox appeals' is testimony to the same point. Charities use Christmas generosity as a spur to encourage donations of basic goods, and indeed some luxuries, to needy children and adults across the world; the need is no doubt as acute in August, but it is apparently harder to encourage British people to give in order to alleviate the need at that time of year.

No-one can deny the good done by such charitable work, or have anything but praise for the staff and volunteers who make many wonderful things happen for very needy people each Christmas season. There is a curious limitation in what we, the British public, will allow in such appeals, however. We are happy to feed and/or clothe someone in need, albeit temporarily; we are much less happy to be invited to question, let alone challenge, the political, cultural, and economic systems that condemn people to lives of desperate need. To take another item from the standard Christmas playlist, 'Do They Know it's Christmas?' was a song recorded by a specially-formed supergroup called Band Aid, organised by Bob Geldof and Midge Ure (who between them also wrote the song), and released in the run up to Christmas in 1984 to raise money for the famine then affecting Ethiopia. The fundraising was extraordinarily successful, particularly through the follow-up concert, 'Live Aid' (held simultaneously in London and Philadelphia, and broadcast around the world, on 13th July 1985). The focus of the appeal, however, was on the alleviation of need; the question of why people in some African nations were unable to support themselves as they had for decades was hardly raised.

The politics of the Christmas we know is limited to giving a goose to Bob Cratchit, or a shoebox of goods to a Romanian orphan, or a few pounds to famine relief; the real business of politics is off-limits. At Christmas we are not permitted to ask why Cratchit cannot afford his own goose, or how Romanian orphanages became overcrowded and underfunded, or what went so wrong as to thrust millions of people into life-threatening poverty in Ethiopia in the 1980s.

The Brazilian Roman Catholic Archbishop Dom Hélder Câmara (1909-1999) famously once commented, "When I give food to the poor they call me a saint; when I ask why the poor have no food they call me a communist." This distinction, between ad hoc occasional political action and determined political theorising, is entrenched and enshrined in our modern British Christmas. We are committed, as a part of our celebration of the season, to giving food to the poor. We are just as determined, however, in our refusal of any discussion of why the poor lack food. Simply put, we don't do politics at Christmas.

chapter 1 references

1. The story is told in detail in S Weintraub, *Silent Night: The Remarkable Christmas Truce of 1914* (London: Simon & Schuster, 2001).

2. Christine Agius, 'Christmas and War' in Sheila Whiteley, ed., *Christmas, Ideology, and Popular Culture* (Edinburgh: EUP, 2008), pp. 137-48.

3. This fascinating episode is discussed in much more detail in Joe Perry, 'Nazifying Christmas: Political Culture and Popular Celebration in the Third Reich', *Central European History* 35 (2008), pp. 572-605.

4. Agius, 'Christmas and War', p. 140.

5. See, e.g., J M Golby & A W Purdue, *The Making of the Modern Christmas* (Stroud: Sutton Press, 2000).

6. See, e.g., Hugh Cunningham, *Leisure in the Industrial Revolution* (London: Croom Helm, 1980), pp. 61-2, recording a story of factory workers requesting a holiday on New Year's Day rather than Christmas Day, because Christmas meant nothing to them.

7. Stephen Nissenbaum, *The Battle for Christmas: A social and cultural history of Christmas that shows how it was transformed from an unruly carnival season into the quintessential American family holiday* (New York: Alfred A. Knopf, 1997).

8. 'Santa Claus' is a corruption of St Nicholas. Nicholas was a fourth-century bishop in Turkey who was renowned for secret gift-giving to the poor and needy of his community.

9. Peter Ackroyd, *Dickens: A Biography* (London: Sinclair-Stevenson, 1990), p. 34.

10. See data quoted from 1969 and 1988, showing almost no shift on this point, in Adam Kuper, 'The English Christmas and the Family: Time Out and Other Realities' in Daniel Miller, ed., *Unwrapping Christmas* (Oxford: Clarendon, 1993), pp. 157-75, data quoted on p. 157.

11. See again Kuper, 'The English Christmas…'; also Mary Searle-Chatterjee, 'Christmas Cards and the Construction of Social Relations in Britain Today', in Miller, ed., *Unwrapping Christmas,* pp. 176-92.

12. Wendy Cope, 'A Christmas Poem', from *Serious Concerns* (London: Faber & Faber, 1992), p. 17; this one collection includes, in a similar vein, '19th Christmas Poem' (pp. 39-40), and 'Another Christmas Poem', p. 74.

a political nativity

We have seen already that our traditional Christmas celebrations have a complex history, but one story remains centre-stage, the story of a birth, in a stable, in Bethlehem.

The claim of the centrality of this story is not as obvious as it might seem. Academic cultural analysis of contemporary celebrations of Christmas can suggest that the recollection of religious themes is accorded a fairly minor place in general. So, Mary Searle-Chatterjee:

> … 'Christian' themes are not, and never have been, of much importance in Christmas cards. For most people the same is true of Christmas in general. Only in primary schools is the Christmas nativity story greatly stressed. Visitors and settlers from ex-British colonies where Christmas is celebrated, comment on the absence of 'religion' in the British Christmas. Communal midnight mass is not central here as it was in Bombay, Goa, or Trinidad.[1]

No doubt many today would accept with little thought Searle-Chatterjee's claim about the essentially un-Christian (she would resist 'secular') nature of Christmas, as conforming to their own experience. We should be somewhat wary, however. The point about card-motifs is correct, but the (unsupported) generalisation to the rest of the Christmas celebration is puzzling. On the one hand, Searle-Chatterjee has acknowledged that cards did not focus on religious themes even when the majority of the population did attend church; on the other, she emphasises at length the preponderance of 'cute animal' motifs on contemporary Christmas cards, a point which surely tells against any easy generalisation from card motifs to wider cultural assumptions about Christmas. Her suggestion that 'primary schools' are the only places that the nativity story is stressed is rather telling: churches generally put some emphasis on the narrative over the Christmas season. According to a ComRes survey conducted for Theos last year, 37% of people in the UK planned to attend a Christmas service. It is difficult to think of another activity engaged in by well over a third of the population that would be invisible to social scientists.

This puzzling invisibility is highlighted by another essay in the same collection, discussing Christmas in Trinidad. Searle-Chatterjee has visitors from Trinidad commenting on the lack of religion in the British Christmas, yet when Daniel Miller analyses the Trinidadian celebration of Christmas, he does so with no mention at all of churchgoing![2] Whatever the cause of this strange blindness amongst a certain sort of academic, there is no doubt that the nativity tableau that is at the heart of the Christmas story remains an image of iconic power (rivalled, perhaps, only by Santa Claus). We need only to note its regular deployment in subverted or ironic ways in advertisements by consciously cool brands, and in contemporary art installations (as, for instance, the controversial 2004 'celebrity nativity' display at Madame Tussauds) to demonstrate this point: at the cutting edge of culture, there remains an assumption that the nativity story is known.

political tales

In fact, of course, most people know the iconic Christmas story well. It is told and re-told every Christmastime, through lisping recitals of half-remembered lines by tea-towel clad children, and in majestic and sonorous tones in cathedral carol services. If a twentieth-century soundtrack of Slade, Bing Crosby, and Band Aid now dominates the shopping centres, the nineteenth-century soundtrack, telling the old story in carols, has hardly been lost. The pure solo rendition of the opening lines of 'Once in Royal David's City' broadcast from King's College Chapel on the afternoon of the 24th December remains a powerful fixed point in the celebration of the season for many, as powerful and fixed, often, as the Queen's speech twenty-four hours later.

The story in its classic form begins with Mary and Joseph engaged to be married in Nazareth. An angel visits Mary, and tells her that, regardless of her virginity, she is pregnant with a child who is God's son, and who will be the saviour of all people. The same angel visits Joseph to convince him to go ahead with the marriage regardless of his wife's pregnancy. Joseph and Mary are forced to travel to Bethlehem to register for a census, she riding a donkey because too pregnant to walk all the way. At Bethlehem, no rooms are available, but they are offered a stable. There, in the straw, Mary gives birth to her son and calls him Jesus. On the hillside above town, angels visit shepherds to tell them about the birth, and they come to visit, carrying a lamb as a present. A star has led three kings from the East to the stable, and they arrive with gifts of gold, frankincense, and myrrh. The story ends with a tableau of shepherds and kings worshiping the new-born baby in his crib, watched by angels and animals. (There might be a coda narrating King Herod's fear of the baby and his slaughter of all male infants in the district in order to kill the child, an intention frustrated by the family's escape into Egypt).

If we take this story as somehow fundamental to the Christmas celebration, as surely we must, and reflect with it in view on the question of the politics of Christmas, then we have to acknowledge that already, in this brief and simple narration, the number of political themes in the story is striking. It is a government census that forces Mary and Joseph to travel to Bethlehem, and that causes such overcrowding in the town that she is forced to

> *Government bureaucracy; healthcare provision; brutal dictatorship; homelessness; asylum seekers; a single teenage mother – with this story in view, it might seem that we simply have to do politics at Christmas!*

use a stable as an antenatal suite. Despite the sanitised images on Christmas cards, it does not take very much thought to realise that a stable is not the most hygienic setting for a birth, and so we can add healthcare provision to the list of themes referenced. Herod is a dictator afraid of his position, and so orders his troops to commit an act of barbarous brutality in an attempt to eradicate a perceived threat. The family is homeless when Jesus is born; their flight into Egypt turns them into asylum seekers. It seems almost certain (given what we know of marriage customs of the day) that Mary was fourteen, perhaps fifteen, and, of course, as the story is told, Joseph is not her child's father: Government bureaucracy; healthcare provision; brutal dictatorship; homelessness; asylum seekers; a single teenage mother – with this story in view, it might seem that we simply have to do politics at Christmas!

This might seem too easy, and we should acknowledge that there is an academic fashion at the moment for re-reading every story as a political text. Given this, we might be rightly suspicious of any proposed political readings of familiar stories. There are philosophers who try to tell us that every reading of every text is irreducibly political, making claims about class and gender and economic distribution that always need to be exposed and challenged. Most writers who argue like this are influenced by a recent continental European postmodern philosophical tradition, sometimes known as 'neo-marxism.' This tradition suggests that competing power-structures lie at the back of every cultural institution and event. A seemingly-innocent story, on this account, reinforces political norms by contributing to a narration of the world in which those norms are assumed to be true. Put very simply, the argument is that if, in every story we tell to our children, men succeed through being violent and women through marrying a prince, then our boys are more likely to grow up being violent and our girls are more likely to grow up assuming that their highest aspiration is achieving a good marriage. Even if we resist such an overwhelming politicisation of our lives – and I think we should – we have to acknowledge that every, or almost every story assumes, and so reinforces, certain political proposals.

Cinderella, on this telling, does in part serve to socialise children into traditional, and oppressive, class and gender stereotypes, not because the story is written or retold to promote such political positions, but because it assumes a world in which they are active, and presents its heroine as succeeding through accepting, rather than challenging, them.[3] Narratives that presume the truth of culturally-powerful assumptions simply do, inevitably, reinforce those assumptions in the minds of their readers. Again, the Wizard of Oz is, according to some readers, in fact a parable of the debate over monetary policy and the gold standard in late nineteenth-century America.[4] The two examples are (deliberately) different: one (Cinderella) suggests that no story is immune from political assumptions and contexts; the other (The Wizard of Oz) that a particular story might be written in order to explore or convey veiled or deliberate political messages. Which is the Christmas story? Is it a narrative that happens to feature government action and policy debates in the background, or does it intentionally offer political analysis and make political proposals?

the biblical stories

To answer this question, we need to go back to look at where the story comes from. The immediate answer, obviously, is 'the Bible,' but in fact the Bible has at least two (perhaps three – I will return to this) different tellings of the birth of Jesus. The composite story I sketched above has elements that are nowhere found in the Bible – including the iconic closing tableau and conflates selected details from the two Gospel accounts of the birth of Jesus in ways which, whilst not necessarily wrong, are certainly added interpretations. It also silently excludes extensive parts of the biblical narratives.

The two undoubted biblical accounts are in two of the Gospels, Matthew and Luke; Luke gives us Nazareth, the angelic visit to Mary, the census, the journey to Bethlehem, the stable, and the shepherds; Matthew gives us the angel visiting Joseph, the star, the wise men/kings (who arrive about two years after the birth), Herod's brutality, and the flight into Egypt.

Luke also has an extensive pre-story involving Mary's cousin, Elizabeth, her husband Zechariah, and their son John, who would grow up to be John the Baptist. The birth of John deliberately parallels the birth of Jesus in various ways: for example, Elizabeth also becomes miraculously pregnant, although in her case the miracle turns not on her virginity but on the (implied) fact that she is post-menopausal. Before the birth of Jesus, Mary and Zechariah both sing remarkable songs of praise to God. Jesus is circumcised on the eighth day of his life, according to custom, and taken to the temple after a month for ritual purification offerings to be made. Matthew has a visit by the Magi, astrologer-priests from the area of modern-day Iran, to King Herod in Jerusalem after the child's birth, but before their visit to Bethlehem. There is also a final angelic visit telling Joseph of Herod's death and instructing the family to return from Egypt. Matthew's account ends with Joseph choosing to settle the family in Nazareth, being afraid to return to Bethlehem because Herod's son is now on the throne. None of these details, from Luke or Matthew, are in the composite story that is traditionally told.

Further, while there are things the two biblical tellings of the story have in common, on the face of it, they look like very different narratives. Matthew says nothing of the birth of John the Baptist, or of a census, a journey from Nazareth, or any shepherds; Luke ignores the kings and the exile in Egypt. There are other details as well: Matthew has the family originally in Bethlehem, and moving to Nazareth after the flight into Egypt and out of fear of continued persecution; Luke has them originally from Nazareth, but temporarily in Bethlehem for the census. For Luke Egypt does not feature; for Matthew it is an important moment in the journey. Both writers present genealogies of Jesus, but the genealogies are strikingly different – they agree on the very early family history, from Abraham down to King David (who reigned a thousand years before the birth of Jesus), but between David and Joseph only two names are shared in the lists, Zerubbabel (who, as governor of Judah, rebuilt the temple in Jerusalem) and his father Shealtiel.

Does this mean the stories are made up? Not necessarily; it does mean, certainly, that the two writers were not trying to produce biographies of Jesus in the modern sense, exploring the inner motivations for his career, and being concerned to offer a complete and historically-accurate narrative. The four gospels are documents which construct narrative worlds, and invite their reader to use the constructed worlds to interpret her experiences. As such, they imply a certain basis in historical fact (the invitation makes no sense unless at least the life, death, and resurrection of Jesus actually happened), but they are less interested in relating a complete set of events in chronological order than in supplying a narrative that offers a compelling vision of the person and teaching of Jesus. The gospel writers want us to know what sort of a person Jesus was, not what a local CCTV camera might have recorded.

Still today we often have legends about acts or sayings of inspirational figures of unconfirmed or dubious authenticity. From one perspective, what matters is not the historical accuracy of the story, but the fact that it captures something of the genius of the person's life, a genius which, caught in a memorable (if unhistorical) phrase or anecdote, can inspire others. With the death of Steve Jobs, many stories illustrating his famous attention to design detail circulated; some were well documented; many more lacked corroboration; some were almost certainly false. For those who told the stories, however, it mattered less whether Jobs really did explore endless varieties of polystyrene packaging, or enthuse in public over the finish of an invisible and inaccessible bit of metal; they were the sort of actions he might well have performed, and they provided for the teller and hearer of the story a powerful and memorable vision of something others in business could and should learn from his approach. That Steve Jobs was something like the person the story portrays, and recognisably so, is vital for the message to hit home; that the details are accurate and verifiable, much less so. Similarly, the gospel writers are concerned to give a vision of the life of Jesus that will inspire and transform their readers: to achieve this they are at least selective, and arguably perhaps occasionally creative, with their material.

If we accept all this, it is still possible to adopt a 'conservative' reading of the two nativity stories. Someone could, that is, claim that all the events described by both Matthew and

Luke in fact happened; the glaring differences are just to do with the two authors selecting different events to make their different points about who Jesus is. Someone else could adopt a 'radical' reading of the two stories, assuming that most or all of the events described are made up in order to convey pictures of Jesus that the authors believe to be true. Equally, someone could adopt a position somewhere between these two. Beyond noting the issue and the possible solutions, the question is not relevant to my argument here, so I will not attempt to solve it.

the purpose of the stories

All this is to say that the two birth narratives are not there to recount bare facts, but to inform us about the significance of the one born. What do they want to tell us about Jesus?[5]

> *The two birth narratives are not there to recount bare facts, but to inform us about the significance of the one born.*

The differing genealogies are perhaps particularly interesting in understanding the different purposes of the authors. Whilst long lists of begettings are tedious and incomprehensible to a contemporary British reader, genealogies played an important part in Ancient Near Eastern cultures, including Israel. We only need to look at the many other genealogical records in the Bible to realise this: being able to list someone's ancestry to many generations actually mattered to these people. Sometimes the genealogy was important to establish a person's membership of the tribe: it functioned almost like a passport or identity card, proving that someone belonged. Sometimes, rather differently, a genealogy served to authenticate a claim to a hereditary office: like a family tree produced by a claimant to the throne during a disputed succession in medieval Europe, it traced the legitimacy of a person's claimed inheritance.

Matthew's genealogy of Jesus is like this latter example: he traces the line of the true kings of Israel, from David down (he assumes that Judah maintained the authentic kingship when Israel split into two kingdoms). Jesus, Matthew wants us to know, is the true king of God's people: his lineage proves it. Luke, by contrast, largely ignores the kings, other than David, but traces the ancestry right back to Adam, the first man 'in Jewish tradition, and the startling and original claim that Adam was 'the son of God'. Luke follows his genealogy immediately by telling of Jesus' baptism, where he says a voice from heaven announced that Jesus was in fact God's son. The claim in genealogy and narrative is that Jesus is God's son.

Matthew's genealogy seems designed to make a political claim, albeit, given the context, a political claim with profound religious consequences. Jesus, he wants to say, is the true king of the Jews. Luke, by contrast, wants to make a theological claim, that Jesus is the true son of God, although his theology has major political implications.

Of course, Matthew is not uninterested in theology: the other big claim of his telling of the birth of Jesus is that Jesus will be *Emmanuel,* which means 'God is with us'. Somehow, he wants to say, the child to be born will mediate the presence of God to the world in a unique way. Matthew peppers his account of the birth with claims that the facts of the birth fulfilled various ancient prophecies, drawn from the Jewish Scriptures, concerning the child to be born (including the famous prediction from the prophet Isaiah, "the virgin shall conceive and bear a son, and they shall name him Emmanuel"[6]). The citation of the prophecies is intended to locate the birth narrative within the ongoing story of God's dealings with the world.

Beyond the linkage with the Hebrew Scriptures, Matthew structures his account to tell his readers all about the child who is born. He begins with the genealogy, answering (for readers of his culture) the question 'who is this child?'; the next section highlights the divine involvement in the birth of Jesus, focusing on angelic visitations, and the virginal status of Mary. This further underlines who the child is: not just son of David, but son of God. (Bethlehem was the ancient city of David, and in telling of the Magi's visit to Jerusalem, Matthew is able to highlight this, further underlining the identification of the child as David's true heir, and so the coming king.) The coming of the Magi highlights another aspect of the story that is worth noting, however: Matthew's focus on foreigners in his story.

It is not just the Magi, trekking from the East, who are a part of this theme's development in the text. In Matthew's genealogy, mostly a traditional list of male heirs, he pauses to mention four women: Tamar, Rahab, Ruth, and "the wife of Uriah" (whose name, we know from the Hebrew Bible narrative, was Bathsheba); the reader is clearly meant to notice these striking additions, and to ponder why these four women (and no others, apart from Mary) are mentioned. Arguably, a part of the reason is that none of the four were Jewish, and so they represent between them, and alongside the Magi, a pointed claim from the author that this is not just about Jesus being Israel's king, the son of David, but about something much bigger, with implications for all the people on the earth (the genealogy, indeed, goes back to Abraham who, according to the Hebrew Bible, was promised by God that "all the families of the earth" would be blessed through his offspring).

Alongside this, we might note that there were aspects of the stories of all four women, and particularly of their union with their partners, that could be interpreted as somewhat scandalous (Rahab, for example, was a prostitute; Bathsheba's relationship with David began in adultery, and David had her husband killed to try to cover up what they had done); given that Matthew's story involves Mary being found to be pregnant before her marriage to Joseph, the reminder that God's providential ordering of David's line had previously invited more than a whiff of scandal was no doubt helpful. Further, all four women took a remarkably – given the cultural assumptions at play – active part in making historically-significant events happen, as does Mary in the gospel narratives.

After all that, however, Herod's fear, and his brutal mass-infanticide, make the point starkly: for Matthew, this birth is a profoundly political event, that threatens established regimes and changes regional power balances (which were delicate, as ever, in the Middle East…). The 2010 BBC serialisation of the nativity story pictured Herod as fearful even of the arrival of the three kings on his territory: the presence of senior political leaders from another land, uninvited, raises questions and demands explanations. The challenging suggestion to God's chosen people that foreigners, also, are implicated in the new thing God is doing, and in central events in their own history, is profoundly political; the gender politics are equally evident, both when Matthew challenges assumptions about appropriate female sexual behaviour, and when he presents his women as engaged in powerful, and divinely-approved, political action.

> *For Matthew, this birth is a profoundly political event, that threatens established regimes and changes regional power balances.*

I will come back to Luke's Gospel in the next chapter, but for now we can see that, for Matthew, this is not just a story with politics happening in the background: this is a political story.

the politics of the stories

The story of Mary, Joseph, and the coming of their first-born, Jesus, is entirely wrapped up in politics. Our Victorian forebears attempted to remove politics from Christmas, to make it a safe time of domestic celebration, untouched by the worrying political, social, and economic challenges of the world outside the front-door of the family home. If Christmas has anything to do with the birth of Jesus, however, this cannot be done. The story is political, through and through.

In particular, in the story of the birth of Jesus, domesticity is completely intertwined with politics. Not just because the child is born to be king, but because the circumstances of the birth, and of the child's early life, are profoundly determined by political realities. If we take the classic composite story, it is no accident that Jesus is born in an outhouse, to parents who are (temporarily) homeless, and without anything like adequate (for the time) medical care. All of this is the result of a political decision, a census called to improve the efficiency (and perhaps, but perhaps not, the fairness) of taxation.

In the face of overwhelming social changes, the British responded in the nineteenth century – but also since   owns grew, and villages depopulated, and mills an   began – as everything in society changed – the Eng   stle, a place of safety with walls built high and drawbridge raised to protect those within against the chaos and uncertainty raging outside. This, the family home, was the place of security and stability, the place where nothing ever changed. Dickens was the greatest, albeit not the only, architect of this place – and Christmas became its festival, the event celebrating the stable and unchanging security of the domestic home, its door locked against the unstable and uncertain world that lay outside.

For Mary, however, politics won't stay outside the door – not the door of the house, and certainly not the closed door of the inn, or the drafty door of the stable. The circumstances of her giving birth, the danger and discomfort she is in, are the direct result of politics. Almost immediately on the classic composite telling of her story, she and her family become asylum seekers in Egypt, because politics intrudes on their life again, as Herod the dictator decides to murder every child in the vicinity rather than let the one that he perceives as a threat live. Only with a change of regime – the death of Herod, and a more benign, or at least more forgetful, policing policy introduced by his successor – can Mary and her family return to enjoy traditional domesticity in their home in Nazareth. Her life story is driven at every turn by political decisions and events.

a political Christmas

The Victorians dreamt that by shutting the door of the family home they could keep politics outside. Christmas was, and apparently still is, the symbol of this dream. That is why we don't do politics at Christmas.

The Christmas story, though, shows that this dream is false: for Mary and Joseph, and for every family before and since, politics gets inside the family home, for good or for ill. If decisions over taxation this year are unlikely to send Mary and Joseph on a long and dangerous trek, with homelessness waiting at the end, they remain likely to influence whether children born into the lowest income decile get anything for Christmas. If we can be confident (in Britain) that we will not see a paranoid tyrant slaughtering children in an attempt to shore up his precarious position, we certainly cannot be confident that we will not encounter the asylum seekers such a tyrant creates, or that their experience of family life – at Christmastime or any other – will not be decisively affected by our political decisions.

What about the couple who find themselves homeless, in our society, even if the cause was not taxation policy? Can we really claim that their domestic experience will be completely unaffected by political decisions? There may be compelling pragmatic or political reasons for the housing of certain homeless families in Bed and Breakfast accommodation, for instance, but one can hardly claim that, for such a family, the experience of domesticity is completely separated from any political decisions or considerations. Again, questions of the level of healthcare available to travellers or the homeless are far from apolitical, and impact decisively on the internal family life of at least some people. It is idle to pretend that traditional domesticity is apolitical.

Even 'traditional domesticity' is a slippery phrase, of course. Across history, and across cultures in the world today, the makeup of families has varied endlessly. If Mary and Joseph really lived without any extended family, that would have been highly unusual for the day. Joseph disappears from the gospel narrative sometime after Jesus' twelfth birthday, suggesting perhaps that he died rather young, leaving Mary to raise, perhaps not Jesus, but certainly some of the younger children, on her own (or, more probably, with the help of extended family members). And of course, on the traditional telling, Joseph is not Jesus' birth father anyway.

We cannot project a vision of the modern Western ideal of the nuclear family onto this narrative. If defence of 'family values' means defending the idea that husband and wife live together with their own birth-children and no others, then the Bible, and not just this story, has no interest in defending 'family values'. (There is, remarkably, not one single example of a nuclear family of this form in the entire Bible, a narrative that spans three continents and two millennia of history.) We need a fairly broad and inclusive account of 'traditional domesticity' before we can begin to imagine that we can claim biblical support for it as a public good.

If the telling of the Christmas story – in the classical form of the nativity play, or in the original form (at least of Matthew's narrative) – is to have any place in our celebration of Christmas, it should challenge us in profoundly political ways. The notion that the domestic sphere is apolitical, unchanging, or even worthy of celebration should be challenged by the telling of this story; the story should bring us face-to-face with our views on homelessness, on asylum, on healthcare provision, on intervention in sovereign states whose authorities are repressing their citizens, on our attitude to foreign people resident in our nation, on our beliefs about gender politics. This is not a comfortable fairy story which silently reinforces traditional values, but a disturbing narrative which confronts us with serious questions about our assumptions concerning the way the world is and should be. This story is, or should be, an insistent intervention in our discussions of the common good, calling us to remember the marginalised and forgotten, to be open to the strange of the foreign. With all due respect to Charles Dickens, the last thing the Christmas story invites us to do is to shut our doors and forget about the world outside.

chapter 2 references

1. Searle-Chatterjee, 'Christmas Cards and Social Relations', p. 182.

2. Daniel Miller, 'Christmas against Materialism in Trinidad', in Miller, ed., *Unwrapping Christmas*, pp.134-53.

3. Jacqueline Wilson, satirising the tradition from the perspective of the child, has Tracey Beaker - the best rounded of a remarkable cast of children she has introduced in her novels - comment bitterly that "[fairy stories are] all the same. If you're very good and very beautiful with long golden curls then, after sweeping up a few cinders or having a long kip in a cobwebby palace, this prince comes along and you live happily ever after." *The Story of Tracey Beaker,* (London: Corgi Yearling, 1991), p. 24.

4. This interpretation was first proposed by Henry Littlefield in 1964, and has often been explored, if not universally accepted, since.

5. We can of course usefully learn many other things from the gospels, and biblical scholarship has often, for instance, focused on looking for hints and details about the communities that these texts were written for and in, or for evidence of the sources used in compiling them; in focusing on the intention of the final-form text, I am not discounting the worth of this, but taking the strand of scholarship most relevant to the question that I am here addressing.

6. The original Hebrew of Isaiah 7:14 has a word that can be translated 'young woman,' not necessarily carrying the implication of sexual inexperience; the gospel writer quotes the Greek translation, which however uses the word *parthenos,* 'virgin'.

the infant revolutionary

So far, I have discussed the traditional composite telling of the Christmas story, how the two biblical narratives fit together, and the politics of Matthew's presentation. Now we turn to Luke's version of the story which, it has to be said, offers a political vision that makes Matthew look rather tame. If Matthew tells a story that challenges us to think about our political presuppositions, Luke's narrative is full of celebrations of direct, and drastic, political change. At one point Luke has Mary proclaiming that "[God]

> *If Matthew tells a story that challenges us to think about our political presuppositions, Luke's narrative is full of celebrations of direct, and drastic, political change.*

has brought down the powerful from their thrones, and lifted up the lowly; he has filled the hungry with good things, and sent the rich away empty." The birth of Jesus, on Luke's telling, is a divine overthrowing of the established political and economic order.

Luke's story

Luke's account of the birth of Jesus is longer and more involved than Matthew's. He begins his gospel (after a brief introduction, addressed to someone called 'Theophilus,' and suggesting that he has investigated various sources to give an accurate portrayal of what happened in the life of Jesus) with the story of a priest, Zechariah, who has a vision of an angel whilst ministering in the Jerusalem temple. The angel tells him that his wife, Elizabeth, previously unable to bear children, will have a son, who is to be devoted to God's service. Zechariah asks how this might be possible, given that he and Elizabeth are both elderly, and is struck dumb until the birth of the child for his effrontery in presuming to question God.

The scene then shifts to Nazareth in Galilee, eighty miles or so north of Jerusalem. The same angel appears to a virgin called Mary, engaged to be married to Joseph, and tells her that she will have a son, to be called Jesus. Mary queries this pronouncement, much as Zechariah had queried the news he heard, pleading her virginity; the angel comments that Elizabeth is already six months pregnant, and that all things are possible with God; Mary acquiesces with her promised/threatened future, and the angel leaves. Mary then visits Elizabeth, whose greeting seems to convince her of the truth of what the angel had said, and she responds with a song of praise, now known as the *'Magnificat'.*

Elizabeth's son is born, and named John, as Zechariah had been instructed. Zechariah is able to speak again, and indeed enabled to prophesy; his prophecy is another song, now known as the *'Benedictus'* (these titles are simply the first word of the songs in the Vulgate, the Latin translation which was ubiquitous in Europe for a millennium). Only after all this do we get the famous story of the census and Joseph and Mary's journey from Nazareth to Bethlehem, and a hint (but little more) of the stable location of the birth: "[Mary] laid him in a manger, because there was no place for them in the inn" we are told. Luke mentions the manger, an animal feeding trough, three times, suggesting it is important; the stable is no more than an inference (although perhaps a reasonable one: where else would an animal feeding trough be the first thing to hand?).

An angel appears to some shepherds on the hillside, soon joined by a full angelic choir, and the shepherds are sent to find the child. They are told that they will know they have found the right baby because they will find him in the manger. They go, and make known what they were told, before returning full of praise for God. The narrative closes with Mary and Joseph performing the approved religious rituals that followed the birth of a firstborn son: Jesus is circumcised on the eighth day, and the family a month or so later attend to the temple to make sacrifices. Whilst in the temple, a prophet, Samuel, and a prophetess, Anna, speak about the future of the child. After the sacrifices, the family return to Nazareth.

Luke's story is less austere in its presentation than Matthew's. The characters in Matthew's story act, and we are told of their (rational) motives, but no indication is given of their feelings, their hopes, dreams, excitements, or fears. Luke's characters, by contrast, are full of perplexity and praise; angelic appearances terrify them (not unnaturally), and prophetic announcements confuse them. Repeatedly, though, the sight of the child quells their fears, answers their puzzlement, and fills them with joy and praise towards God.

That said, we should not make the mistake of finding modern concerns of characterisation in Luke's story. He is not giving us clues to inner psychological states; rather, he is picturing ideal responses by a cast of characters who represent true piety as depicted in the Hebrew Bible. They are poor and oppressed people, living under foreign occupation, but faithful to God and looking with confident expectation for God to bring salvation to them. For Luke, this promised salvation is irreducibly political and economic in character: when God's promised salvation comes, poor and oppressed people will be liberated from their poverty and oppression. The coming of Jesus into the world is the key moment in bringing this divine promise to fulfilment. Luke's Christmas story is therefore wrapped up in an expectation of political transformation. To understand the power of this, we need to understand the political context of the day, and also to understand some of the religious expectation that shaped the experience of that context for at least some of the people.

a context of political oppression

At the time of the birth of Jesus, Palestine had been under foreign occupation almost continually for nearly six centuries. Jerusalem had fallen to the Babylonian Empire in 586 BC, and had then been successively conquered by the Persian Empire, Alexander the Great's Macedonia, and two of the Hellenistic kingdoms that resulted from the break-up of Alexander's empire. The second of these, the Seleucid kingdom (which conquered Palestine in 198 BC), had been brutal and repressive, the regime culminating in widespread religious oppression and the flagrant desecration of the Jerusalem temple. This, inevitably, led to a revolt in the mid-160s BC. Surprisingly, perhaps, the revolution achieved some success, and for a few decades the land enjoyed at least some measure of independence under a dynasty of kings called the Hasmoneans. The kingdom was always precarious, however, and Rome finally annexed it in 63 BC.

Roman rule in Judea was harsh, albeit perhaps not intentionally so. Both client-kings (such as Herod the Great) and Roman governors (such as Pontius Pilate, whose reign came after Judea was made a province rather than a client state) have reputations in the histories of the time for casual brutality. Herod embarked on an ambitious programme of civic improvements, which must have stretched his kingdom's economy, particularly given a severe drought and famine during his reign. (The Romano-Jewish historian Josephus writes of a delegation sent to Rome after Herod's death requesting a reduction in the tax burden, who complained that Herod "reduced the entire country to helpless poverty".[1]) In typical fashion, subsistence farmers, who made up most of the population, were reduced in bad years to borrowing the foodstuffs they needed to live, often at exorbitant rates of interest. There were numerous revolutionary movements in the middle decades of the first century AD, fuelled, according to Josephus, by a pervasive sense that the burden of taxation was unjust and unbearable. This unrest culminated in the revolt of 66 AD (crushed by Rome in AD 70). Revealingly, one of the first acts of the revolutionaries was to burn the public records of debts owed. The people certainly felt that they were being slowly crushed by taxation and usury, and the evidence we have suggests that they were right to feel like this.

In this context, Luke's narrative of a casual upheaval of families in order to put taxation records into order is frighteningly plausible (indeed, we have records of something very similar happening under Roman rule in Egypt in 103 AD[2]), as is Matthew's account of a casual slaughter of a region's male children to stamp out a possible political threat. This is not all background context, however. Luke chooses to be very direct in his political location of his story. His narrative of the birth itself (after the stories of the two miraculous pregnancies) begins with a decree issued by "Emperor Augustus"; almost immediately angels appear to the shepherds on the hillside announcing the birth of a "Saviour" who will bring "peace".

We are so accustomed to thinking of Jesus as a "saviour", and giving that word a safe religious meaning, that the oddness of the title is easy to miss. In fact, the title is ascribed to Jesus only twice in the four gospels (here, and in John 4:42), and is not much more common elsewhere in the New Testament. It was, however, a standard title applied to imperial rulers, and particularly to Augustus. As the one who brought an end to decades of constant warfare in the eastern empire, Augustus was widely and routinely hailed as the saviour who had brought peace to the world. Inscriptions to this effect were common across the Eastern Mediterranean region, and it is difficult to believe that we are not meant to hear some echoes of this imperial claim in the angelic proclamation. Luke's hailing of Jesus as 'saviour' comes so quickly after a reference to Augustus that the use of the title seems obviously pointed, and the following claim about the establishment of peace must have been equally recognisable. If Matthew has the local client-king worried about the coming of a potential rival in the birth of this child, Luke has the heavens proclaiming that Caesar's salvation and peace is a sham, which will be exposed and replaced by this child.

We should not be too quick to spiritualise this into an account of the replacement of a political and military order with a spiritual and ethical order. In imperial Rome, and still more in the eastern part of the Empire, religious devotion and political obedience were inextricably intertwined: emperor-worship was common, and the worship of Rome itself, under the guise of the goddess Roma, became institutionalised in the east in the first century BC. For Luke and other eastern imperial Christians, the idea of a political order that was not also religious, or of a religious order that was not also profoundly political, would have been so far from anything they knew as to be almost inconceivable. If the peace of Christ will expose the *pax Romana* as a sham and replace it, that will necessarily be, if not a political event, then at least an event with significant political implications.

For shepherds on a Judean hillside, there can be little doubt that Caesar's 'peace' and 'salvation' was little more than a sick joke. Bethlehem was famous as an area where livestock farming predominated (for the straightforward reason that the soil was too poor for much arable farming), and so these shepherds are simply, and recognisably, representatives of the vast mass of the local people. The experience of the poorest in the client states and colonies of Rome was a life of routine oppression and brutality. A hefty tribute to Caesar was demanded on top of all the local demands for taxation; any suggestion of disloyalty (including a delay in paying the tribute) would result in exemplary punishment on a large scale.

Around the time of Jesus' birth, there were several messianic movements in Palestine that were perceived as threats by the Roman overlords. In response, the entire city of Sepphoris, which was only a few miles from Nazareth, was razed, and its inhabitants enslaved. In Judea, two thousand people were crucified, their dying and dead bodies lining the highways. This was the reality of Caesar's peace and salvation. The best an ordinary farmer or shepherd could hope for was that, with a bit of luck and decent weather, one might keep one's head down and scratch a bit of a living whilst avoiding being caught up in any concerns of the invaders.

poor and faithful people

Luke's picture of God's deliverance being announced first to these ordinary subsistence farmers, rather than to priests or kings, is characteristic of his vision of how God works. At the beginning of the adult ministry of John the Baptist and Jesus, Luke writes, beautifully, of the various rulers around, and of their utter irrelevance to what God was doing:

> In the fifteenth year of the reign of Emperor Tiberius, when Pontius Pilate was governor of Judea, and Herod was ruler of Galilee, and his brother Philip ruler of the region of Ituraea and Trachonitis, and Lysanias ruler of Abilene, during the high-priesthood of Annas and Caiaphas, the word of God came to John son of Zechariah in the wilderness. (Luke 3:1-2)

No doubt part of Luke's purpose here is to locate the event historically: dating by years of reigns was common. The first clause contains all that would be needed for a date, though: "the fifteenth year of Tiberius" is enough. The piling up of names of emperors and governors and rulers and high priests provides a biting comic context for the final announcement: God is at work in the desert, not in the palaces or temples; kings and priests are no part of what God is doing; indeed, they are bypassed by it. God's word comes to John the Baptist in the wilderness, a representative of the ordinary people, of the faithful poor.

> *God is at work in the desert, not in the palaces or temples.*

There was a long tradition in the Hebrew Scriptures of the piety of the faithful poor. This was perhaps particularly marked in the Psalms, the ancient songs of praise that were collected and included in the Hebrew canon. The psalmist would acknowledge his need for help on account of his poverty, but protest that his hope is only in God, as in the opening words of Psalm 86:

> Incline your ear, O LORD, and answer me,
> for I am poor and needy.
> Preserve my life, for I am devoted to you;
> save your servant, who trusts in you.

The context of such protestations is normally an experience of opposition (in the same Psalm, consider verse 14: "O God, the insolent rise up against me; a band of ruffians seek my life…"), and often a direct experience of political oppression, as at the beginning of Psalm 10:

> Why, O LORD, do you stand far off?
> Why do you hide yourself in times of trouble?
> In arrogance the wicked persecute the poor…

The shepherds, and all the other subsistence farmers and bonded labourers who made up the vast majority of the population of Palestine, and who suffered under Roman oppression, and from the careless demands of local rulers, stood in direct continuity with a major strand of the spirituality of the Hebrew Bible. When they called out to God for deliverance, they were echoing an ancient and oft-repeated prayer. And the testimony of their ancient Scriptures was that God always hears the cry of oppressed people like them. It is no surprise, then, that the coming of a promised saviour was a looked-for moment that would bring political and economic transformation to the land.

I mentioned above the surprising focus on the manger, the feeding trough, in Luke's account of the birth of Jesus. It is mentioned three times in a brief passage, suggesting that it is important. If we look for symbolism, it is hard to find. Perhaps, however, the meaning of the manger is more direct: for shepherds and others, a newborn child put to rest in an animal's feeding trough would obviously be 'one of us,' someone who is born into the world of struggle for survival and precarious existence that is the common experience of the people.

The BBC production, *The Liverpool Nativity,* that re-set the story in contemporary Merseyside, and used songs from Liverpudlian groups to narrate it, finished with an image of the new-born Jesus put to bed in a shopping trolley. This image was undeniably powerful, but I wonder if it missed the point slightly. Anyone who has lived and worked in deprived communities in Britain knows well the practice of using a drawer as a bed for a newborn child, a free alternative to buying a crib or Moses basket that will be used for a few weeks only. Perhaps the manger functioned like that: for ordinary people, a kid who sleeps in a drawer, or a manger, can be seen to be one of us, not one of them, the feared, hated, and despised ruling classes.

In the Hebrew Scriptures, ordinary people, suffering under unjust rulers, became the central image of true piety. The person who has come to the end of her own resources, and so cries out to God, is the person whose spirituality is to be commended. Further, the promise is held out that God will act to deliver her. This is emphatically not a promise of rewards in the afterlife that would, somehow, make up for the suffering endured in this life; it is a promise that God would overthrow the oppressors and set the oppressed free.

Luke repeatedly references this promise, and believes and claims that in the coming of Jesus, the promise is fulfilled. The coming of Jesus is the overthrow of the oppressive political order and the establishment of a new order that, in political and economic terms, will be better, more just, for the suffering people. Perhaps the most telling example of this theme is the songs that Luke records, songs that echo phrases and themes from earlier songs of praise from the Hebrew Bible, but which also rejoice in the new thing that God is doing in the birth of Jesus. And in these songs this new thing is, inescapably, political.

songs of freedom

Mary's song, the *Magnificat*, stands first, and is the most powerful expression of this theme. The song echoes several traditional songs of praise in the Hebrew Scriptures, but draws the echoes together into a satisfying literary whole of its own. Mary begins by praising God, because, seeing her trouble and poverty, God has intervened. God is holy, and so merciful to those who wait faithfully for deliverance; equally, God's is mighty, and has acted to overthrow the oppressors. The 'proud' are scattered; the 'powerful' are removed from their thrones; the 'rich' are dismissed with nothing. In contrast, the 'lowly' are lifted up, and 'the hungry' are filled. God has helped the people, in accordance with the ancient promises.

In the song of Mary, the salvation that God brings is entirely political. Mary associates herself with her people, speaking of her 'lowliness' (the Hebrew parallels are all of women who found themselves unable to bear children, and so were disgraced in their society; as a young teenager, this cannot be true of Mary, but her song takes the older language of disgrace and re-applies it to the political situation of the people). Those who reign are rich, powerful, and proud; they will be cast down and sent away with nothing. They, ironically, will go hungry for a change, while Mary's people, shepherds and subsistence farmers and artisans and bonded labourers, will be lifted up and filled. The vision is so direct that it could come straight out of a communist tract of the 1930s; social revolution will exalt the proletariat at the expense of the ruling classes.

For Mary, and for Israel, however, this is not the work of some ineluctable and universal force of history, as it was for Marx; rather it is the direct intervention of the God who has made them the chosen nation, and who now will step in and save them. There is nothing in the song, we should note, that suggests that this is a vision of some distant action of God in the far future, some final bringing of justice at the end of time. The birth of the child is the moment of change, not some imagined moment in the future. When he grew up and began his ministry, Mary's child would say "Blessed are you who are poor, for yours is the Kingdom of God; Blessed are you who are hungry now, for you will be filled…" (Luke 6:20-21). This, as his mother's song, is concrete and immediate and economic and political.

Zechariah's song, the *Benedictus* (Luke 2:68-79), again celebrates God's bringing salvation to the people, and also the preparatory role that Zechariah and Elizabeth's son John will play in that ("you will go before the Lord to prepare…", v. 76). The song is perhaps less obviously political than the Magnificat, but the political references and expectations are still there if we understand the context of the language. Much of the song speaks of concepts such as salvation and redemption, which obviously could have a political reference. When we consider the political context of foreign occupation, such phrases as "saved from the hand of our enemies and from all who hate us" (v. 71) are probably most naturally read as a promise of overthrow of the current political order. Again, in choosing to recall "the oath [God] swore to our ancestor Abraham" (v. 73), the lyric seems to be deliberately referencing political hopes: the promise given to Abraham had two parts: that his children would grow into a populous nation, and that they would own the land in which he was no more than a tolerated immigrant. God's remembering of this promise must be understood as an expectation that control of the land would be returned to the people, and so that the occupying forces would be expelled.

The final song in Luke's narrative is sung by Simeon in the temple when the child is brought for the purification rituals. Known as the *Nunc Dimittis,* it is found in Luke 2:29-32. Simeon is a very elderly man, who is said to have been waiting for "the consolation of Israel" (v. 25). He blesses the child with words of cheerful resignation, suggesting that now that he has seen this child he is happy to die. Simeon's brief song again speaks of the coming of Jesus bringing God's deliverance. It is followed, however, by a prophecy that "this child is destined for the falling and rising of many in Israel…" (v.34), suggesting again that God's deliverance would at least include widespread political and economic upheaval in the nation.

learning from Luke's nativity

Luke's account of the birth of Jesus seems to deliberately draw attention to the context of Roman occupation, and to the political and economic oppression the people are suffering as a result. Jesus is carefully painted as a member of the oppressed populace, despite his ancient pedigree as the heir of King David. The coming of Jesus will bring salvation for the people, but this salvation cannot be limited to a religious experience; rather it will include political transformation, the freeing of the land from its oppressors.

If Luke's account is more pointedly political than Matthew's, it is also harder to draw direct contemporary political application from Luke than from Matthew. We do not, thankfully, live in a context of foreign imperial oppression, and so a nativity story that is in part about God's response to such oppression is not directly applicable to us. Luke does, however, challenge some myths that remain popular today, as they were in the time of the early Roman empire: that armed invasion might be a successful means of bring peace, for example, or that invading a foreign nation can be a way of 'saving' its people. His straightforward account of the human suffering caused by bureaucratic decisions designed (in this case) to streamline the system of tax collecting might also serve to give us pause for thought.

Luke's nativity is not a story that is designed to make policy proposals. Rather, it is an exposé of the difficult lives of ordinary people under oppressive regimes, and - fundamentally – a suggestion that God cares about such troubles; indeed, that God cares enough to act in decisive ways to change the lives of faithful people who suffer.

Perhaps the fundamental political message, addressed indifferently to politician, tyrant, or bureaucrat, is that you too will be held accountable for your decisions and actions, held accountable largely on the basis of whether you helped or hurt the people under your control. In the UK, as in most Western democracies, we benefit greatly from a political class who are generally devoted to public service; where this is not the case, Luke's story stands as a blunt warning.

salvation, promised and political

This is not, of course, the whole story for Luke. Jesus' coming will change many things, freeing his people from their sins, for instance. Our question here is political, however, and the politics of the story are obvious and inescapable. The coming of Jesus is the coming of a new order that will threaten the old order, clash with it, and finally overthrow it. I indicated in passing above that there is, perhaps, a third biblical telling of the birth of Jesus. The highly allusive and symbolic final book of the New Testament, Revelation, was almost certainly written in a context of active persecution of the early church by the Roman Empire, and it presents this persecution through a series of pictures, drawing on well-recognised mythological elements, that were designed to encourage the readers to believe that, improbably (indeed, miraculously), the outcome of the conflict would be the triumph of the church and the end of Empire. At one point in the book we read this:

> A great portent appeared in heaven: a woman clothed with the sun, with the moon under her feet, and on her head a crown of twelve stars. She was pregnant and was crying out in birth pangs, in the agony of giving birth. Then another portent appeared in heaven: a great red dragon, with seven heads and ten horns, and seven diadems on his heads. His tail swept down a third of the stars of heaven and threw them to earth. Then the dragon stood before the woman who was about to bear a child, so that he might devour her child as soon as it was born. And she gave birth to a son, a male child, who is to rule all the nations with a rod of iron. But her child was snatched away and taken to God and to his throne… (Rev. 12:1-5)

The language here is like the symbolic language of political cartoons: the cartoonist can present a grotesque vision of an eagle, and expect the readers to understand that the United States of America is meant, for instance. The dragon is named as the devil in verse 9, but portrayed here as an evil empire: many-headed and many-horned monsters wearing crowns are a staple image for empire – here, presumably, Rome. The woman can be understood as an image of the church, and the persecution the church has to endure; however, the assertion that her child is destined to "rule all the nations" invites us to see here also an account of the birth of Jesus.

In typical political cartoon style, all subtlety is forgotten here, and the scene is presented as one of naked conflict. The child threatens the established political order, and so is to be devoured even as he is born. He escapes, however, and war ensues. In this stylised cartoon version, the birth of Jesus is a nakedly political moment. Neither Matthew nor Luke will go this far, but both will insist on the genuinely political nature of the event.

The Christmas story, in its biblical presentations, is not narrowly political, but that does not mean it is not still profoundly political. It describes how political realities impact ordinary lives. It speaks of God's willingness to act to change unjust political structures. And it affirms how, improbable as it may often seem, the way of things can – and will, one day – be transformed.

chapter 3 references

1. Josephus, *Antiquities*, 17.
2. See Richard A Horsley, *The Liberation of Christmas: The Infancy Narratives in Social Context* (New York: Crossroad, 1989), p. 71.

the politics of Christmas

We don't do politics at Christmas. Under the tutelage of our Victorian forebears we have made it a celebration of a mythical and stable British family life, seasoned with a certain amount of charitable donation. Christmas is a time for the family to gather, and for the door to be shut against troubling political questions and developments.

As I have noted, however, it was not always thus: before the Victorian period, and sometimes locally for many years beyond the assumed triumph of the new vision, an unquestioned and comfortable domesticity was not on the table – and if the biblical narratives of the birth of Christ are to be our guide, nor should it have been.

> *The nativity stories present a stark warning: God is interested in political matters, particularly as they concern those who are most vulnerable.*

The nativity stories challenge our traditional celebration of Christmas with the thought that domesticity and politics are not opposed, particularly for the poorest and most vulnerable in our, or in any, society. They offer us quietly-stated but powerful testimony to the truth, perhaps obvious once stated, that political decisions inevitably affect, and often transform, our experience of family life. This was the experience of Mary and Joseph, travelling the hard road from Nazareth to Bethlehem, and finding the promise of communal deliverance and salvation there. It is the experience of anyone committed to living in the light of that story now or in the future.

Further, for those who find in the biblical narratives an account of the ways and works of God, the nativity stories present a stark warning: God is interested in, and concerned about political matters, particularly as they concern those who, through poverty, or oppression, or plain bad luck, are most vulnerable. Understood on its own terms, the nativity story is a testimony of profound significance that this God is interested in politics, and even prepared to get involved in politics, coming in the person of the Son to challenge the imperial rulers whose actions, whether motivated through brutality or ignorance, lead to the poorest experiencing oppression. God is present, and God is active; therefore, somehow, injustice will end. This was the confident expectation of those involved in telling the Christmas story from the first.

Should we do politics at Christmas? The question is more: how, seriously, can we avoid it? At least, how can we avoid it if we pay any attention to the story on which our Christmas is ultimately based? The nativity story is many things, but it is certainly, amongst them, a powerful human drama of how the lives of ordinary people can be disturbed and destroyed by political systems and decisions, and how God cares and interferes in these affairs to "fill the hungry with good things." Nativity plays and carol services are not – or should not be – safe, comfortable, 'feel-good' moments through which we escape from reality, but rather occasions of truth and hope, where the faithfulness of God breaks through into the ordinary, where we are invited to consider how God intervenes in the business of politics.